P9-APE-610

This is Your Brain on

ANXIETY

What Happens and What Helps

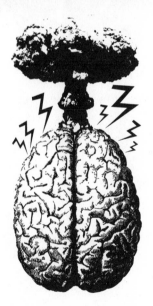

FAITH G. HARPER, PhD, LPC-S, ACS, ACN

Microcosm Publishing
Portland, OR

THIS IS YOUR BRAIN ON ANXIETY

What Happens and What Helps

Part of the 5 Minute Therapy Series
© Dr. Faith Harper, 2016, 2018
This edition © Microcosm Publishing, 2018
First edition, first published 2016
Second edition, first published March 14, 2018

ISBN 978-1-62106-421-3
This is Microcosm #205
Cover illustration by Meggyn Pommerleau
***To join the ranks of high-class stores that feature
Microcosm titles***, talk to your local rep: In the U.S. **Como**
(Atlantic), **Fujii** (Midwest), **Travelers West** (Pacific), **Brunswick** in Canada, **Turnaround** in
Europe, **New South** in Australia and New Zealand, and **Baker & Taylor Publisher Services** in
Asia, India, and South Africa.

For a catalog, write or visit:
Microcosm Publishing
2752 N Williams Ave.
Portland, OR 97227
www.microcosmpublishing.com

If you bought this on Amazon, that sucks because you could have gotten it cheaper and supported a small, independent publisher at MicrocosmPublishing.com

Microcosm Publishing is Portland's most diversified publishing house and distributor with a focus on the colorful, authentic, and empowering. Our books and zines have put your power in your hands since 1996, equipping readers to make positive changes in their lives and in the world around them. Microcosm emphasizes skill-building, showing hidden histories, and fostering creativity through challenging conventional publishing wisdom with books and bookettes about DIY skills, food, bicycling, gender, self-care, and social justice. What was once a distro and record label was started by Joe Biel in his bedroom and has become among the oldest independent publishing houses in Portland, OR. We are a politically moderate, centrist publisher in a world that has inched to the right for the past 80 years.

Global labor conditions are bad, and our roots in industrial Cleveland in the 70s and 80s made us appreciate the need to treat workers right. Therefore, our books are MADE IN THE USA and printed on post-consumer paper.

Library of Congress Cataloging-in-Publication Data

Names: Harper, Faith G., author.
Title: This is your brain on anxiety : what happens and what helps / Faith G.
   Harper, PhD, LPC-S, ACS, ACN.
Description: Portland, OR : Microcosm Publishing, 2018. | Originally
   published: 2016.
Identifiers: LCCN 2017014396 (print) | LCCN 2017025891 (ebook) | ISBN
   9781621065814 (ebook) | ISBN 9781621064213 (pbk.)
Subjects: LCSH: Anxiety disorders. | Anxiety disorders--Treatment.
Classification: LCC RC531 (ebook) | LCC RC531 .H37 2018 (print) | DDC
   616.85/22--dc23

CONTENTS

INTRODUCTION

When you struggle with anxiety, the most empowering thing in the world is realizing that you aren't weak, broken, or batshit crazy.

I'm not just saying that to placate you. It's scientifically true. Anxiety makes perfect sense because it's how our brains are wired to protect us. Certain mental health issues, anxiety being one of them, are the direct result of how we have evolved for survival. Certain memories are stored in certain ways in order to protect you. When those memories are triggered, rational thought gets bypassed and your body goes into **do something to fix this** mode. (If you wanna nerd out more on the brain science stuff, you should totally read my other book, **Unfuck Your Brain**.)

If you're still reading, that probably means that your brain regularly gets hijacked by anxiety. And you're over that shit. And you want your life back. So here's what we're going to talk about:

1)   What anxiety actually is. You know, as opposed to all those other emotional states (fear, depression, etc.) That seem all vaguely interconnected but have a lot of differences in terms of what's going on in the brain and how we can best manage them.

2)   The whole brain science/brain chemistry aspect of how anxiety is triggered.

3)   The **how to deal with it** part. Both in the middle of an attack, and more generally over the long term.

4)   How to cope when you also have to deal with other people, relationships, jobs, schools, etc. Anxiety wouldn't be so bad if it wasn't for other people in your life, right?

5)   How to provide support if someone you care about has anxiety. Because that's just as helpless a feeling as having anxiety yourself.

Has anyone ever told you "You should try yoga! Or meditation! Or keep a thought diary! Or spin in a circle three times when a bell rings!"

Sometimes (ok, a lot of times) people will suggest something because they read about it, or tried it themselves, or saw other people try it and that it helped. But when you're in the midst of feeling anxious, you look at any option and think, **can this actually help my anxiety? And if so, how is it actually helping?**

We all get to a point where we are tired of spinning around when the bells ring in hopes of feeling better.

So along with the **this is the why shit's fucked** portion of the book, I'll explain the **why** part again with the **fixing it** part. Like "this is helpful because it counteracts this chemical in your body with this other one" or "this is helpful because it helps unpack thinking habits that tend to reinforce anxiety and we're gonna try to break that cycle."

Seeking the rationale behind whatever I'm doing, or working with clients to do, has made me a better therapist. It's definitely made me a healthier person. We should never swallow everything we're told as absolute truth. So, I did my research, figured out why things worked, and figured out ways sometimes to make them work better. That's how this book came into existence.

If you are nodding your head in agreement? You're gonna get as much out of reading it as I did out of writing it. And I'd love to hear from you about it. You can email me at theintimacydr@gmail.com

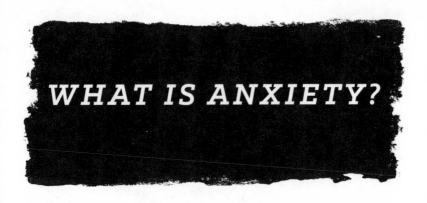

WHAT IS ANXIETY?

Don't you just love dictionary definitions? Anxiety is…
the state of being anxious.

Well, no shit.

As a nerd is wont to do, I looked up the Latin root of the word "anxious." It's ***anxius***, which comes from the word ***angere.*** Which means "to choke." Fucking word gets that right.

Interestingly enough, the word "anxiety" (and its definition of "being anxious") isn't one bit modern. In fact the word "anxious" was used MORE in the early 19th century than it has been in the early 21st.

You know what that means? Anxiety is a human condition that we have been grappling with for centuries.

To be sure, modern living is stressful as hell. But modern life is not the source of human anxiety. Humanity in and of itself is an anxiety-provoking experience for so many people.

The psychologist Rollo May noticed this huge societal movement toward anxiety long before I did.

His work as an existential therapist in the middle part of the 20th century focused substantially on the problem of human anxiety. He didn't have Google algorithms to tell him the word popped up in the 19th century and has been a thing ever since. But he was a fucking brilliant scholar of philosophy, and he totally grokked from those readings what was going on.

A major philosophical shift in how humans viewed themselves started in the 19th century. This was a movement towards **technical reason**: the idea that our best decision-making occurs when we are detached from our emotional reactions. This was a new thing. In the 17th century, the big philosophical idea was one of **rational reason**: the belief that even though you have emotions, you should make rational decisions for your life and not let those emotions control you. Technical reason, on the other hand, suggests that emotions have no place in decision-making at all. Instead of honoring the existence of emotions, people came to believe we should repress them.

So as Rollo May oh so dryly noted in his book ***The Meaning of Anxiety,*** *"In view of this psychological disunity, it is not surprising that anxiety should have emerged as an unavoidable problem in the nineteenth century."*

So I mentioned above that May was an existentialist. This means he believed that reason is not the source of meaning. And that meaning-making in general cannot be universalized. **Meaning is unique within each of us.** He was a follower of Kierkegaard in believing that our true vocation in life is to be our unique selves. So it makes sense that when being our unique selves is denied to us on such a huge cultural level, anxiety occurs.

I think there is a lot of truth there. BUT. There is more to it than that.

The whole field of psychology is based on the worldviews of European and European-American men with significant educational privilege and at least some level of financial privilege.

Being an educated white guy is by no means a background that protects you from anxiety, but you may experience anxiety in a different way than most other people. If you are an academic or researcher, your background will also shape how you theorize what anxiety is and how to manage it.

Then, in the 1970s, there was a pretty huge shift in the theoretical work of mental and emotional health. Something we now call Relational Cultural Theory (RCT) started being written about and talked about by women in academia. Women like Jean Baker Miller and Carol Gilligan had different experiences of privilege and different ideas about what wellness would really entail for the rest of us. There were two main ideas in their work that were hella fucking radical at the time, but make nothing but intuitive sense 50 years later. They are:

1) Human beings are hardwired to connect. We get better in healthy relationships and crave interdependence, not independence. But our general ideas about mental health are still focused generally on being independent rather than relating with others to support our wellness.

2) We are the products of all sorts of fuckedupedness. If your world is disrupted on a regular basis because of who you are, what you look like, and where you live, you lack privilege in those areas. And lacking privilege makes you far more susceptible to mental health issues and less likely to receive appropriate treatment for them.

What they were pointing out was not only had our entire culture shifted to one in which the prevailing idea of emotions was that they are total bullshit and have no place in decision making, but that we've also had huge shifts in how people perceive the importance of relationships. And the gaps between groups with privilege and groups without have gotten larger.

Emotions matter. Privilege matters. Relationships matter. And we live in a time where all these things are HUGELY disrupted. Rollo May had been the first to glimpse that historical shift when looking at how philosophical thought was changing throughout time. Short answer: these disruptions have been happening at warp speed since the dawning of the Industrial Age. In the 19th century.

It's really fucking hard to tolerate uncertainty, disruption, and change in all aspects of one's life at once when you don't even know exactly who you are and who you are supposed to be.

And when SO much is going on, it's too big to fear. Fear is specific. It is outward in the fact of a threat. When you fear something you have the opportunity to move away from it.

Anxiety is different. With anxiety, you don't know what the fuck to do, because it's all internal. **There is no specific threat.**

Which is why the symptoms of anxiety cover so much ground. At its coolest setting, it can be the experience of unease. At medium heat, it's distress. At a full boil, it's straight up panic. And as those ancient Italians well knew, it's a hugely somatic experience. That is, it's something you feel in your body as much as something that controls your thoughts.

And it's the most uncomfortable feeling ever. Your body is intentionally making you feel off balance so you have to attend to it. There's a fancy term for that: **Disequilibrium**.

So here is our working definition: Anxiety is a state of full body disequilibrium at a level of intensity that demands immediate attention and corrective action on your part. It can be in the face of a real or perceived threat, either present or anticipated.

That right there is why anxiety is so hard to ignore. The whole point of the body producing that feeling is to demand your full attention like a naked, raging toddler running through the street in a snowstorm with a fist full of gummy bears in one hand and a bloody machete in the other.

Quite a visual right? Sure as hell not something you can readily disregard in the course of your day.

Anxiety demands every ounce of attention we have, no matter how inconvenient the time or unnecessary the anxiety actually was to begin with. If you have the kind of history that tells you to constantly be on guard, it's really easy for anxiety to be the default setting.

Anxiety Really Does Sound a Lot Like Stress

Yup, totally. And anxiety often comes from chronic stress. The big difference? Stress has external triggers. I know, I know, so does anxiety, but hang with me.

Stress can produce anxiety, but it can also produce a ton of other emotional responses (depression is probably the biggest). Anxiety is an internal response to stressors.

Think of it as a workflow process. If stress, then anxiety. Or any other number of uncomfortable emotional states. It all happens so fast it ends up mashed together in our brain. But there is definitely a cause and effect thing going on between the two.

A good book if you are interested in learning more about this is **Why Zebras Don't Get Ulcers** by Robert Sapolsky.

So Where Does this Anxiety Shit Come From?

Generally speaking, the human body works hard to maintain its chill point. So why is the body intentionally making you all bonkers-batshit with this anxiety thing? That makes as much sense as cheerfully banging your head into a brick wall, dunnit?

It all comes down to brain wiring.

Short version: We are wired to have strong emotional responses because those responses keep us alive. Feeling anxious is absolutely an important survival skill.

Longer version: If something triggers an anxiety response, your body gets flooded with norepinephrine and cortisol. Here's what those do:

Norepinephrine is released through your central nervous system (Hah! Nervous!) in order to prepare your body (which includes your brain) for action. It increases your focus and attention as well as your blood flow, blood pressure, and heart rate.

Cortisol is the classic stress hormone. It increases blood sugar and suppresses the immune system. Many people with chronic stress also gain weight, specifically as "belly fat," due to the constant cortisol production. The important thing to know here is that when cortisol is released with its partner in crime, norepinephrine, it creates strong memory associations with certain moods, to create warning signals of what you should avoid in the future.

The interesting thing here about anxiety as a stress response? The good thing? Anxiety means the body is still fighting back. This is fundamentally different from depression, which is essentially a wired response of learned helplessness (this is Robert Sapolsky stuff again).

Anxiety symptoms are active coping skills in the face of threat. The problem is only when the brain has decided that most everything is a threat.

WHAT ANXIETY FEELS LIKE

Thoughts and Feelings Symptoms

· Excessive worry

· Rumination (hamster wheel thinking patterns)

· Irritability/anger (Weird, right? Anger is the culturally allowed emotion so we substitute that one a lot for what we are really feeling.

· Irrational fears/specific phobias

· Stage fright/social phobias

· Hyper self-awareness/self-consciousness

· Feelings of fear

· A sense of helplessness

· Flashbacks

· Obsessive behaviors, pickiness, perfectionism

· Compulsive behaviors

- Self doubt
- A sense that you are "losing it" or "going crazy"

Physical Body Symptoms*

- Trouble falling asleep or staying asleep
- Inability to rest
- Muscle tension
- Neck tension
- Chronic indigestion
- Stomach pain and/or nausea
- Racing heart
- Pulsing in the ear (feeling your heartbeat)
- Numbness or tingling in toes, feet, hands, or fingers
- Sweating
- Weakness
- Shortness of breath
- Dizziness
- Chest pain

- Feeling hot and cold (feeling like having chills and fever without running a temperature)
- Shooting pains/feeling like you have had an electric shock

You are probably reading the physical body checklist and thinking... this is the same list for everything from anxiety to Ebola. Which is why so many people end up in emergency rooms thinking they are having a heart attack when they are having an anxiety attack. It's ALSO the same reason many people have missed the fact that they were having a heart attack because they were also having an anxiety attack. In Mental Health First Aid training (mentalhealthfirstaid.org), we suggest that if you see someone with potential anxiety attack symptoms, you ask them if they know what is going on and has it happened before. If they say "no" then treat it like the potential emergency situation it may be and call 911.

Of course there are tons more symptoms. These are the more common ones and a complete list of all the things you may experience with anxiety would be an entire pamphlet of list-ness. You can find lots of great lists all over the interwebz, including ones that break down all the different categories of anxiety symptoms.

A lot of other things we do are adaptive to managing anxiety as well. Obsessive-Compulsive Disorder is totally an anxiety response. Cutting and other self-injury behavior may not stem from anxiety in all people, but it does for many. So many diagnoses out there stem from just a few core issues. Anxiety is totally one of them.

But yeah. Anxiety symptoms. There is a lot of nasty shit our bodies do to us to get our attention and make us correct course.

Any of those hit home? You probably aren't reading this if the answer to begin with was "Nah, I'm always chill."

DO I HAVE ANXIETY OR AM I JUST ANXIOUS SOMETIMES?

You ask the most awesome questions! Like any other mental health issue, the answer lies in whether or not anxiety is controlling your life, rather than being a legit way of your body telling you to get off your ass and do something.

Clinically speaking, if you say it's a problem, I will agree that it's a problem. You know you the best.

Some people want a more formal way of self-check. There are a lot of anxiety assessment scales out there. The one you see quite often is the OASIS (which stands for Overall Anxiety Severity and Impairment Scale). It's well backed up by research and it's free to use, since it was developed by the National Institutes of Health (NIH).

OASIS doesn't have a magic cut-off number (as in: below this you are fine, above this you are batshit anxious). But it can be a good starting point for opening a conversation with a treatment provider or even just to reflect on your experiences.

The OASIS questions ask for you to reflect on your experiences over the past week and rate them on a scale of 0-4, with 0 being no probs, 1 being infrequent, 2 being occasional, 3 being pretty frequent, and 4 being constant fucking companion, thanks for the reminder.

Yeah, I'm translating a bit there. You can see the entire scale with the exact wording online, download it and print it if you want. (http://tinyurl.com/jnubjvx)

The exact questions themselves are as follows:

· In the past week, how often have you felt anxious?

· In the past week, when you have felt anxious, how intense or severe was your anxiety?

- In the past week, how often did you avoid situations, places, objects, or activities because of anxiety or fear?

- In the past week, how much did your anxiety interfere with your ability to do the things you needed to do at work, at school, or at home?

- In the past week, how much has anxiety interfered with your social life and relationships?

Having a "holy shit that's me!" moment? You are so not alone. The Kim Foundation notes that about 40 million American adults ages 18 and older (18.1 percent of people) in a given year meet the criteria for an anxiety disorder and 75% of individuals with an anxiety disorder had their first episode before age 21.

WEEKLY MOOD TRACKER

AM I IN A BAD
MOOD OR...
DO YOU SUCK?

	MOOD	SITUATION	MAGNITUDE (0–100)	SYMPTOMS
SUNDAY				
MONDAY				
TUESDAY				
WEDNESDAY				
THURSDAY				
FRIDAY				
SATURDAY				

DEALING WITH ANXIETY

Sometimes we know straight up what our triggers are gonna be.

We know a first date or a public speaking engagement or a meeting with our boss is going to send our anxiety through the roof. We know a road trip where we can't find a clean rest stop with a non-sketch bathroom is gonna cause a freak out (And why is there NOT an app for that??? The struggle is REAL).

But sometimes? Not a fucking clue. Like all other mental health issues, we may have a genetic predisposition to anxiety and/or it may be a product of the environment we grew up in or live in now. And that can make figuring out our specific triggers difficult.

A mood tracking diary (either an app or old school paper one) feels like a lot of work, but can really help with figuring out your triggers. You can use the super-simple template on the facing page. If you need help figuring out the exact right word to describe what's going on in your body, do an Internet image search for "feelings word wheel."

Any of the exercises in the next section can be used to help manage anxiety in the moment. Give your anxiety a goofy name or persona. Carry ice to hold as a reminder. Do some deep breathing exercises.

And then, when you aren't feeling anxious, you can work on longer-term self-training to rewire your brain.

Disrupting The Signal: Short-Term Anxiety Management

Even once you've figured out your triggers, anxiety isn't something you can willpower your way out of.

As you saw, we have the asshole twin chemical combo going on. So in the here-and-now moment of anxiety or a straight up panic attack, you gotta do something t metabolize out those chemicals. When anxiety hits, you have to fight it head on.

Here is some stuff to try:

1) **Deep Breathing and Progressive Relaxation.** Yeah, yeah. That shit is hard to fucking do when you are spun up. But it's important to at least try. Because the chemicals released during an anxiety or panic attack are designed to get your breathing ramped up and your heart racing. So it's going to add to the sense that you are going to have a heart attack or that you will stop breathing. Of course, that isn't going to happen. Try reminding your brain and body about that. Making a conscious effort to breathe and un-tense will slow the heart rate back down and help you get more oxygen flowing. It's a literal chemical counter-balance. Want detailed instructions for this? They're in the next chapter.

2) **Name That Bastard.** Give your anxiety an actual persona to inhabit. Name it after a heinous ex, a shitty grade school teacher, or Kim Jong-un. Create a whole character for your anxiety. Anxiety feels so nebulous that giving yourself someone to battle really helps. Then you can have convos with Donald Trump's Epic Hair Swirl (or whomever, but personally I think all panic attacks should be named after that hair) whenever it comes calling. You can focus on that entity the way you would an actual person that was threatening you in a real-world situation. You can negotiate, you can yell back, you can lock it in a box. Whatever works.

3) **Create Coping Cards.** Coping statements are pretty much as simple as they sound: Mantras or reminders that help you manage your anxiety and stay in control of your body. They can be literal self-talk ("This will only last a minute") or a reminder to take a deep breath. You know,

whatever helps. But the problem with coping statements is you sure as fuck aren't going to remember them in the heat of the moment. When you find mantras, facts about anxiety, or other statements or images that help you, put them on an index card. Hole punch those and put them on a snap-shut key ring and you have a set of coping cards you can flip through when panic hits. It sounds epically nerdy, I know. But I have had so many clients end up loving the shit out of their cards and using them all the time.

4) **Ride The Wave.** Avoidance is what makes it worse. Try setting aside 5 minutes to sit with the anxiety you're feeling instead of fighting back. It won't last forever, I swear on my Roomba it won't. If you attend to what you are feeling, you get over it way more quickly than if you avoid it. I've noticed I'm bored with myself about 3 minutes into committing to sitting with my feeling for 5. I'm ready to go make a cup of coffee, read a book, find the cookies I hid from myself, or do anything other than perseverate.

5) **Put it On Ice.** We used to encourage clients to wear a rubber band and snap it on their wrist if they felt an urge to self-harm, or were having spinning thoughts, or considering an impulsive behavior. But, um, snap a rubber band on yourself enough times and you will tear the fuck up out of your skin. So we're not doing that anymore.

But the point of the rubber band was legit. We were trying to help people disrupt the current focus of the brain by encouraging it to attend to another pain point. Ice works much better without causing lasting damage. Seriously, try it. Grab an ice cube and squeeze. Your brain is gonna be all "OW! WTF you doing that for??" and it disrupts the signal. If you have an impulse to self-injure to manage anxiety, you can actually place the ice on the part of the body you typically hurt instead of doing the other harm behavior.

The cool thing too, is carrying ice with you isn't obvious. You can bop around in your day, and grab an ice cube out of your cup without people going "What the hell is that about?" I have worked in group programs where everyone carried water, so handing someone a water cup full of ice to use if they got triggered didn't make them feel singled out to their peers.

Longer-Term Self-Training

Like all other brain retraining, there are certain things that can really help combat chronic anxiety. It isn't a magic bullet, better-immediately type cure, but the idea of training yourself to be optimistic has some merit behind it. There is a guy named Martin Seligman who is a legit big deal in my field. He was studying learned helplessness when he noticed that there are certain qualities that those obnoxiously, cheerful Susie-Sunshine optimistic people generally have:

Permanence: Optimistic people don't dwell on bad events, and approach them as temporary setbacks. If they get neg'd on, they bounce back more quickly. They also believe that good things happen for reasons that **are** permanent. Essentially, the world is fundamentally in their favor.

	Adverse Event #1	Adverse Event #2	Adverse Event #3	Adverse Event #4	Adverse Event #5
Adversity					
Belief					
Consequences					
Disputation	Evidence? Alternatives? Implications? Usefulness?	Evidence? Alternatives? Implications? Usefulness?	Evidence? Alternatives? Implications? Usefulness?	Evidence? Alternatives? Implications? Usefulness?	Evidence? Alternatives? Implications? Usefulness?
Energization					

Pervasiveness: People who are happy monkeys tend to keep failure in its proper place. They recognize failure in one area as only belonging in THAT area, rather than meaning they are a failure at ALL THE THINGS ALL THE TIME. They also tend to let the things they are good at inform the rest of their lives, rather than keeping that in its own space. Sucking at basketball doesn't mean you will now make a shitty risotto. And if your risotto rocks, it is an indicator that YOU rock. And that you should cook more often. And invite me for dinner, I love risotto.

Personalization: Our cheerful buds blame bad events on bad circumstances rather than bad selfhood, but take good circumstances as indications that they are good people. So basically failures are events, not people. But successes are people, not events. If you dig me?

Interested in figuring out which way you wire? You can take the Learned Optimism test at http://tinyurl.com/hpwls4m

Understanding what makes an optimist gave Seligman an idea. If we can learn helplessness and pessimism, then why can't we learn optimism and a positive outlook? Especially if we know the three big indicators we are shooting for? Let's start with challenging our Neg Gremlins.

Take Action: Challenge Your Neg Gremlins

Seligman created an ABCDE model designed to help you reframe your thinking as optimistic. And yes, it looks a ton like Albert Ellis' Rational Emotional Behavior Therapy (REBT) and Aaron Beck's Cognitive Behavior Therapy (CBT). We all borrow from each other's shit all the time. Therapists and researchers are assholes like that.

Think about the last time you felt anxious and write down some notes for each of these five letters:

In Seligman's model the A stands for Adversity. What bullshit is going down that generally triggers your anxiety response?

B stands for Belief. What are your beliefs about this event? Be honest, if your anxiety is triggered a lot, you are probably running a thought pattern in the direction of "THIS SITUATION IS FUCKED!" Beliefs just mean your **thoughts,** how you interpret what happened. Not your emotional responses. It may also be a flash of a memory, rather than a fully-formed thought, if the situation triggered a trauma response.

C stands for Consequences, though really it should stand for Cookie. Seligman didn't agree with me that once you think that shit's fucked you should go have a cookie. Instead, he wants you to look at how you reacted to the situation and to your beliefs. This is where your **emotional responses** (how you felt) go, as well **as what you did/how you behaved.**

D stands for Disputation. This is where you literally argue with the neg-gremlins your brain is throwing down and focus your attention on a new way of coping. Create a new story to use instead.

And finally, E stands for Energization. What was the outcome of focusing your attention on a different way of reacting? Even if you were still pretty anxious, did you handle the situation better than you may have in the past? Over time, with doing this, do you notice that your anxiety is starting to fizzle out FINALLY?

To start with, just fill out the first three categories (A-B-C). Think back and look for examples of pessimism and negativity. Highlight those instances. Did you beat yourself up way more than you expected?

Give it a few days to sink in and then sit down with this list again and add the last categories (A-B-C-D-E). This is gonna be harder—this is active work to challenge that pessimism and teach yourself optimism instead. But you got this, rock star. It takes practice, so stick with it!

1. **Adversity:** Just the facts, baby. Describe what happened (who, what, where, when) being as precise and detailed as you can.

2. **Beliefs:** What were you thinking? Like, exactly. What was your self-talk? Don't care if it was crude, ugly, or weird. Write it down. If it sparked a memory or flashback, that counts, too!

3. **Consequences:** How did these thoughts affect how you felt? How you behaved? What went on in your body? What emotions did you experience? How did you react?

4. **Dispute:** There are four different ways you can dispute these negative beliefs:

A. **Evidence?** Is there evidence that your belief is based in reality? If someone says "I hate you," then the belief that they hate you has some evidence behind it, right? But most beliefs really don't.

B. **Alternatives?** Is there another way you can look at this situation? What were the non-static circumstances (you don't always bomb a test, so maybe you were overtired from being sick)? What are the specifics (sucking at basketball doesn't make you a lame human being or even a lame athlete)? What did others contribute to the situation (is it really ALL your fault???)?

C. **Implications?** Ok, so maybe you fucked up. Is it really a total catastrophe? What's some perspective you can add (If I failed in that job interview...that doesn't mean no one will hire me from now to infinity)?

D. **Usefulness?** Just because something is true doesn't make it useful. How can you frame the experience as one that gives meaning to your life? Do you have a better respect for those things or people you value? Can you better demonstrate that respect now?

5. **Energization**: How do you feel post-disputation? Did your behavior change? Your feelings? Did you notice anything within the problem that you didn't notice before? Maybe even created a solution?

Now go celebrate your success here, hot stuff! By doing this work on yourself, you start extinguishing anxiety as your go-to response because you don't see the world around you as so much of a threat.

That's not bad, eh?

MORE SHIT THAT HELPS

Deep Breathing. When I work with kids I call it belly breathing. When I work with vets, police officers, and first responders I call it tactical breathing. The official term is diaphragmatic breathing or abdominal breathing which are just the most ridiculous words ever...I swear to Buddha, we must make this shit up just to see if we can get people to follow along.

So if you have seen any of those terms it's totally all the same thing. And all it really means is that you are taking in your breaths by contracting your diaphragm, which is a muscle that lies horizontally across your body, between your abdominal cavity and your thoracic cavity.

Sounds complicated? Not so much. You totally know how to take a deep breath. It's when your belly moves instead of your chest. You get far more oxygen in your blood when you are breathing in this manner, which will disrupt the anxiety response. Have you ever been so anxious that you felt light headed and about to pass out? Your breathing was likely totally to blame. You weren't breathing in a way that gave you the oxygen you need to manage your anxiety response.

If you want to practice this, lie down and put something on your belly. Your favorite stuffed animal, your unopened growler bottle, whatever. You should see it move while you breathe.

Yup, that's it, you got it.

Try to focus on your breathing instead of the other bullshit chatter that your brain is insisting you pay attention to. Counting helps, too. Try these counts for breathing in, holding, and breathing out.

Only count as high as you can comfortably go. You aren't gonna get graded on your breathing and it isn't meant to be stressful. If you're asthmatic, have allergies, etc., anything more than 6 seconds may be literally impossible. No sweat, OK?

Breathe In and Count To	Hold and Count To	Breathe Out and Count To
3	3	3
3	3	6
6	6	6
6	6	9
9	9	9
9	9	12
12	12	12

Passive Progressive Relaxation

Now we are going to work on relaxing each part of your body moving progressively down. This isn't one of those exercises where you tense up first so you can then relax yourself and feel the difference. That's a useful exercise on other occasions, but not when you already fucking know you are tense and don't need anything else making you more tense.

If it helps you to have prompts, you can find lots of guided progressive relaxation exercises on YouTube.

Start with the deep breathing. You know how to do this part now, so you can move the teddy bear or growler. Lie down, relax, and lay your arms and hands, palms to the earth, down to your side next to you. Close your eyes if that feels safe and comfortable for you.

Start at the top of your head. Tune in, beginning with your crown, moving slowly down your scalp. Feel your ears relax.
Feel your temples relax, and then your brows.
Feel your eyes relax, then your cheeks, then your nose, and then your mouth. Relax your lips and your tongue.
Feel your throat relax. Then your neck.
Feel your shoulders relax. Focus on letting them drop everything they've been holding for you. They get to rest, too.
Focus on your right hand. Let the calm flow from your right shoulder, down your arm. Through your wrists, then into each finger. Start with your thumb and move through each finger to your pinky, relaxing every digit.
Now focus on your left hand. Let the calm flow from your left shoulder, down your arm. Through your wrists, then into each finger. Start with your thumb and move through each finger to your pinky.
Now focus back on your shoulders, and let the relaxation flow through your chest down into your belly. Your belly is moving gently as you continue deep breathing, but otherwise has no other work to do right now. It doesn't have to hold itself up or in with any tightness.

> Go back up to your shoulders, and let the relaxation flow down your upper back to your lower back. You've been holding a lot there, haven't you? Maybe the entirety of the world. You don't have to, at least for right now. Let it go for a while.

> Relax through your buttocks, through your root chakra, and down through your hips. Let the calm flow down through your thighs.

> Move down to your knees, then your calves.

> Move down to your ankles. Your feet. Let yourself relax each toe. Start with your big toe and move to your pinky toe.

Once you feel ready, open your eyes and slowly get back up again. You may feel a little sleepy, or woozy, or fuzzy. That's OK. Take your time rejoining the world and remember what relaxed feels like. You're allowed to feel that way!

Exercise. I know, I know. Fuck Crossfit and fuck spinach smoothies. But exercise releases endorphins. Short version of that? Endorphins have mad ninja skills... they block our perception of pain and enhance positive feelings...both of which counterbalance the stress response. Which means those superfit people who say they get a runner's high? Totally aren't lying. Freaks of nature, maybe. But telling the truth.

You are allowed to choose a form of exercise you can tolerate. I am not a fan of sweating and physical exertion in the name of health. But my doctor keeps telling me that reaching for a cookie does not count as a sit-up, so I gotta do SOMETHING. I do enjoy swimming, walking, and hiking... they are way more relaxing and meditative for me than competitive team sports (but if that's your thing... go on with your weird-ass self!). Even better is when I go hiking with my bestie. We get exercise and get to talk about shit in the process.

Find something that doesn't suck. It can be as intense or gentle as you want, but try stuff. Most places will offer a free class or free week so check shit out. I had a client who fell in love with boxing by trying out a free class. It was great exercise AND made her feel more empowered and in control of her experiences.

Meditation. No saffron robes need, I promise. But meditation releases dopamine, serotonin, oxytocin, AND endorphins. And it's cheaper than Crossfit. 6000 years of Buddhist practice has something going for it, yeah?

Here's my recipe for mindfulness meditation:

Sit upright. If you can do this without back support, like on the floor on a cushion then good on you. If you need a straight back chair, do that. If you can't sit at all, that's OK, too. Get yourself in whatever position is most comfortable. The reason sitting is better than laying down is that the point is to fall awake, not fall asleep. But the point is also to not be in screaming fucking pain, so don't stress it.

Soft-focus your eyes so they aren't closed but they are seeing without actually seeing. You know what I mean. Be visually spaced out because what you are really going to be paying attention to is inside you.

And now you are going to breathe in and out. And focus on your breath. If you have never done this before it's going to be weird and hard.

But for the record, if you have done this a zillion times chances are still good that it will be weird and hard.

If you catch yourself being distracted, just label it "thinking" and go back to focusing on your breath. Thinking isn't a failure in the least. It's gonna happen. And noticing it and bringing the mind back to the present moment is the point. So it's a total win.

Treat your bodily reactions like any other random thought. Itching is common. If you catch yourself itching, label it thinking three times before succumbing to the urge to scratch. You may be surprised at how often your brain is creating things for you to focus on. Of course, if you have real pain, don't ever ignore that. Rearrange yourself for comfort and don't be a hero.

A lot of people feel awful during meditation, thinking they suck at it because they are continuously distracted by chatting thoughts. That's OK. Your brain is desperately seeking to story-tell. All kinds of distracting stuff is going to come up. You are going to think about what you need to cook for dinner. Or a conversation you had at work. Or whether or not you should buy new sneakers or go to a movie this weekend.

I'm not even going to pretend that this shit is easy to do when you are spun up. But it's important to at least try. Because part of a panic attack is the stories our brain starts telling us about the attack itself. And it's generally not a pretty story. The chemicals released during an anxiety or panic attack are designed to get your breathing ramped up and your heart racing. So your brain starts insisting that you are going to have a heart attack or will stop breathing. That's not going to happen. When you catch that thinking, remind yourself that's a biochemical response, but not reality.

And here is the thing about mindfulness meditation… research shows that it disrupts the storytelling process of the default network. We used to think the only way to do that was a distraction by outside events and stimulus, but the opposite works, too.

So keep breathing. The continued, conscious effort to breathe and un-tense will slow the heart rate back down and help you get more oxygen flowing. It's a literal chemical counter-balance. And it gives your brain the space it needs to tell itself new stories.

Touch. Give someone a hug. Go get a massage or a pedi. Get acupuncture or acupressure or another kind of treatment that involves touch. Cuddle with your boo. Touching and being touched releases oxytocin. Touch is also good for the heart and the immune system. So if it's ok for you to do, get on that.

Get Yourself Outside. Sometimes the doing of anything feels like way more than can be handled. Remaining vertical is difficult enough, there certainly isn't going to be any meditation or exercise or any other woo-woo shit.

If you can't do anything else, try to get yourself out in some sunshine. Even if it's just to sit on a bench while drinking your afternoon coffee or something. Sunlight increases vitamin D production and serotonin. Both of which will give you a little chemical boost without having to pop a pill. It's hard to sit in the sun and feel like ass at the same time. And trust me, I've tried. I usually perk up despite myself.

If you live in a grey and gloomy place, you may want to invest in a personal sunlight lamp that you keep on your workspace. When my brother left Texas to go to school on the East Coast, he found himself battling seasonal affective disorder (SAD). He just wasn't getting enough sunlight to battle a low-level blues. The lamp made a huge difference.

Seeing a pattern yet? If anxiety is a chemical reaction, then the cure is to counteract that shit. Asshole chemicals are best fought by our happy chemicals. And since I can't convince science that coffee and cookies are happy chemicals, we have to go with dopamine, serotonin, oxytocin, and endorphins. And while Vitamin D isn't a chemical like the rest, a lot of people don't process it well in their gut and find they feel so much better when they seek out more of it from sunlight.

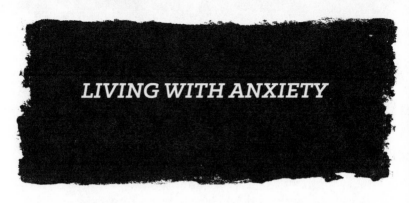

LIVING WITH ANXIETY

The brilliant thing about anxiety is it allows us the opportunity to anticipate and plan how to manage life.

The complete fuckitude of anxiety is it allows us the opportunity to anticipate and plan out how to manage life IN ALL THE FUCKING HORRIBLE WAYS IT CAN GO WRONG AT ALL TIMES AND UGH JUST FUCK IT ALL IN THE EAR I'M GOING BACK TO BED.

So how? How do you do any of it? How do you do this life-ing thing when your PJs are far more comfortable than any other clothing you own and it's all such bullshit, anyway?

Mostly, because you want to, at least at some level. And it's worth it, at most levels.

Here's what you do:

1) ***Self care.*** We've been talking about this. The thing is, you have to keep doing it. Like all the fucking time. Getting better doesn't mean stop doing the things that got you better, right? It's like tossing the antibiotics before you finished the whole course of treatment. Except the whole course of treatment may be taking care of yourself gently for the rest of your life. And you're allowed to. And supposed to. Keep up with that.

2) ***Talk about it.*** Talking about it doesn't mean emotionally vomiting all over everyone. It means explaining your reactions. Something like "Do you read Jenny Lawson? I'm totally having a Blogess anxiety moment right now. I'm not trying to be an asshole, but today has been fucked for me. I'm gonna go grab some water and be back in a second." Boom, it's that easy. It's amazing how supportive people can actually be if you give them the chance. If you try to talk to someone and they are dismissive and unempathic, then

they are either total assholes (and fuck them) or they are dealing with their own shit and don't know how to be there for you (so fuck them, at least for now).

3) **Ask for help.** Because, seriously. It takes far more courage and strength to ask for and receive help than it does to give help. Give people a chance to help you, but give them that information in very specific ways like "Can you come sit with me at my doctor's appointment/come with me to walk my dogs/meet with me for coffee and discuss the complete mindfuck **The OA** was for me?" And if they say no, then we are back to saying, fuck them. You were brave to ask. Keep asking. And think of it like any other ATM. But with help instead of cash. You put in help when you have it to give, and you take out help when you need it.

4) **Create.** That Rollo May dude I was talking about? He cited interesting research that shows that the best way to manage anxiety is to first be able to sit with it. Which

makes sense. If you can't even tolerate it, you certainly won't be able to find ways to manage it. And the research shows that creative people are the best at finding ways to sit with it. So get creative. Write it out. Make art. Putting things out there in the world helps us be more authentically who we are. Anxiety and all.

5) **Know your rights.** If you are in work or school and your anxiety is super batshit, you do have legal protections if you need accommodations and if your employer has 15 employees or more. Federal law requires you to try to figure out how to resolve any problem and request a reasonable accommodation. You will likely have to provide documentation of your anxiety diagnosis. But you can't be fired for outing your anxiety and asking for your desk to be moved to a quieter location, or something else entirely reasonable. You can see more about ADA rules here: https://www.eeoc.gov/facts/fs-ada.html

Being a Friend to Someone with Anxiety

This can be tough, right? Even if you have anxiety yourself and you totally get it. When you are relying on someone but they are all up in their struggles and can't be there for you. When you don't know what the fuck is going on, just that they are checked out.

It's OK to ask, it's OK to talk about it, and it's OK to be there for them in whatever ways works for y'all.

Say, "Hey what's up. I haven't seen you in a while (or plans were canceled, etc.). Do I have halitosis you aren't telling me about or did I piss you off without intending to? I know your anxiety can be bad sometimes and I was wondering if that was something you were struggling with and if so I'm available to talk about it/not talk about it/help in any way I can."

It's OK to be upset if their anxiety is fucking over your plans, too. But own it for exactly that. Your friend already feels shitty enough. So say, "Yeah, I was bummed that you didn't show up last night. I love spending time with you. If your anxiety is that bad right now, should we try for different kinds of plans? Or do you need to tell me when you want to do stuff so you don't feel pressured to hang out when you really don't want to?"

Offer to help them with their progressive relaxation or deep breathing. Offer to go for a walk with them, or to a yoga or meditation class. Deposit into the help ATM for when you need it later.

CONCLUSION

So what do we do with all this? Do these coping skills make anxiety all magically, immediately better?

Of course not. And anyone who offers a super quick cure in that regard is an epically shitty, false-hope peddler. Without understanding what's happening, anxiety is just an epically shitty experience followed up by a mindless attempt at treatment.

But now you have a new weapon: The "why."

Your brain is busting its ass to protect you and keep you safe. It's just gone off-the rails out-of-control in trying to figure out what to protect you from. And it's impossible to control something we don't understand. The why things are happening part helps make the fixing it part actually work. That's been my experience. And the experience of most everyone who I've ever talked to about anxiety. Likely your experience, too.

Anxiety is a motherfucker. I'm not about to lie to you in that regard. All the things that make us brilliantly, wonderfully, amazingly human are the exact same things that make us prone to this diffuse, unpindownable sense of anxiety and dread. And the world we live in is a bubbling cauldron of shit to be anxious about.

But when it comes down to it, the existentialists like May and Kierkegaard were **right**. The more we are able to fight for **ourselves**, for our unique humanity and individual reasons for being, the more we win. And the more the anxiety inside us settles down. And the more the anxiety that surrounds us doesn't consume us. We have to fight for ourselves and fight for the people we love.

We have to do it even when we are anxious.

Fucking hell, **especially then**.

All these skills, all these ways of supporting your struggles with anxiety? Think of them as your personal rebel alliance fighting for your right to survive. There will never be anything else you do that is more radical than investing in your own self-worth and self-care.

A COUPLE OF THE BOOKS I SHOUTED-OUT HEREIN

Why Zebras Don't Get Ulcers by Robert Sapolsky

This book is totally about the body as a biological machine and explains why humans are more susceptible to stress-related diseases (like, you know, anxiety) than animals are. The last chapter is more self-help oriented. But if you like to nerd out on the science part, this book is the schizz. (Sapolosky is also heavily featured in the National Geographic documentary ***Stress: Portrait of a Killer***. Last time I looked, it was up on YouTube.)

The Meaning of Anxiety by Rollo May

May was smart AF, y'all. And an amazing philosopher as well as a clinician. I think he missed out on many of the ways lack of privilege can affect anxiety but it doesn't mean that many of his ideas weren't brilliant and a good starting place. And hey, he was a well-educated, well off white dude in the middle 20th century, so not exactly an intersectional feminist (and, TBF, relational cultural theory didn't even EXIST yet) so I give him a pass on that end. It's still a good grounding if you are interested in the historical underpinnings of anxiety.

Toward a New Psychology of Women by Jean Baker Miller

Jean Baker Miller's theories about mental health looked at how stereotypes have shaped mental illness. She took what all of the institutional ideas about power, success, strength, and autonomy really mean and turned them on their head.

In a Different Voice by Carol Gilligan

Gillian's work molded neatly with that of Miller's even though they were not working together at the time they were researching and writing these books. Gilligan was focused on looking at human development through a new lens, instead of only the current theories available regarding mental health. Her interest was in the space that lies between experience and thought, and how those things shape and inform each other. Her use of the word "voice" to replace the notion of "selfhood" is something that I have carried forward in my own research.

Learned Optimism by Martin Seligman

If we can learn helplessness, we can learn the reverse, right? Fuck yeah, that's right! Human beings are wired to the negative as a protective mechanism that doesn't serve us super-well in the long run. Seligman uses classic cognitive therapy techniques with a twist to show people how to rewire their brains into more positive thinking and responses.

Furiously Happy: A Funny Book About Horrible Things by Jenny Lawson

Jenny Lawson (The Bloggess) writes about surviving the whole host of disorders she has struggled with, including depression and anxiety. She walks that balance of not taking it all so seriously and taking it VERY VERY seriously. It's a fine line, isn't it? She does the thing. This makes it possible to laugh and relate and actually feel better without disrespecting the seriousness of what you're going through.

What About Bob?

No matter how bonkers you are feeling, Bob has it worse. I have had so many people tell me that movie made them feel way sane…in a good way. Both my kids call it their favorite movie ever. Best part is that Bob epically wins at life in the end. Hope for us all!

As Good As It Gets

Melvin has hardcore OCD. If you consider OCD as an adaptive response to society for someone who has tons of anxiety, his way of navigating the world makes so much sense. He also wants to get better. He is an utterly grouchy ass who is also totally lovable.

The Perks of Being a Wallflower

Charlie has a trauma history and a lot of tough experiences in high school. He's also an introvert struggling with understandable anxiety. In the end he decides to be more engaged in his life, stating: ***"Even if we don't have the power to choose where we come from, we can still choose where we go from there."***

High Anxiety

Mel Brooks did a funny spin-off on Hitchcock's Vertigo. Madeline Kahn describing anxiety is well worth the You Tube search in and of itself.

SUBSCRIBE TO EVERYTHING WE PUBLISH!

Do you love what Microcosm publishes?

Do you want us to publish more great stuff?

Would you like to receive each new title as it's published?

Subscribe as a BFF to our new titles and we'll mail them all to you as they are released!

$10-30/mo, pay what you can afford. Include your t-shirt size and your birthday for a possible surprise!

microcosmpublishing.com/bff

...AND HELP US GROW YOUR SMALL WORLD!

More Five Minute Therapy: